This is simply a great book! Inspirational, scholarly, informative and easy to read. The reader will be able to "see" the Image of the Invisible God clearly on every page! Jacob Hawk is not only a great preacher...he's a great writer!

Kent Allen
Vice President for Advancement,
Oklahoma Christian University

Today we have "pop theology", and lots of "feel good" writing about religion. What we don't have is the message of heaven faithfully translated into modern words and thought patterns. Jacob Hawk's new book solves that problem by skillfully blending the ancient and the modern. When you finish the book, you have no need for someone to separate the message from its bondage to modern culture. The Bible's thoughts about God are delivered with startling clarity. Pulpit ministers will find it a gold mine of freshly dug sermon ore. The people in the pew will find themselves able to vividly see in Jesus what they have not seen before; that is, the invisible God.

Robert K. Oglesby, Sr.
Pulpit Minister, Waterview Church of Christ

In recent months, one of my private longings has been to know more about God the Father and draw closer to him and his Son Jesus Christ. To help me focus on this goal, I searched for writings in my library, catalogs, and bookstores. Providentially, I believe, Jacob Hawk's manuscript about "The Image of the Invisible God" came into my hands. It has refreshed my spirit and reminded me that Jesus is the image of God and that God's desire for me is that I imitate Jesus in my life. To know Jesus is to know God; to become like Jesus is to become like the Father. This is spirituality in its purest form.

Jacob Hawk provides suggestions to help readers turn their backs on the false images the world extols and imitate Jesus Christ who is "the image of the invisible God."

Howard W. Norton, Ph.D.
Former president of Baxter Institute
Tegucigalpa, Honduras

Image

of the

Invisible

GOD

Image
of the
Invisible

GOD

JACOB HAWK

TATE PUBLISHING
AND ENTERPRISES, LLC

Published by Tate Publishing & Enterprises, LLC
127 E. Trade Center Terrace | Mustang, Oklahoma 73064 USA
1.888.361.9473 | www.tatepublishing.com

Tate Publishing is committed to excellence in the publishing industry. The company reflects the philosophy established by the founders, based on Psalm 68:11,
"The Lord gave the word and great was the company of those who published it."

Book design copyright © 2013 by Tate Publishing, LLC. All rights reserved.
Cover design by Allen Jomoc
Interior design by Jomel Pepito

Published in the United States of America

ISBN: 978-1-62746-678-3
1. Religion / Christian Life / Spiritual Growth
2. Religion / Biblical Studies / Jesus, The Gospels & Acts
13.07.18

Dedication

To my precious son, Hayden—may you
always grow in the image of God.

And to my beautiful wife, Natalie—thank you
for your godly faith that reflects the Father.
You make me want to reflect him more.

Table of Contents

Chapter One

Perplexing Paul

It was a beautiful day, but to me, it was simply depressing. The sun was shining, the birds were singing, and the beauty of God's creation was bursting at every corner, but where was I? Sitting at my desk, in my office that was quickly becoming a dungeon.

In my worn leather chair, I stared at piles of sermon ideas that lacked imagination and character. My soul was burdened by the stress of ministry, my energy flirting with the cooling flame of burnout.

Where was my passion? Where was my drive?

Satan was winning. The presence of God was disappearing, and my joy was fading like the heat of the distant sun.

I pushed aside my feelings of defeat and fixed my eyes back on my calling. I was a minister of the gospel of Jesus Christ, a proclaimer of the "good news." Like John the Baptist, I was a "voice of one calling" for anyone to listen.

Not in the desert, in the Texas Hill Country, but my message was the same, "Make straight your paths for the Lord!" The congregation needed a word from the Lord, and I had been chosen by God and hired by man to give it, but Satan was tearing apart every creative idea, and I sat helpless with nothing to say.

But as my hands turned the pages of the Bible, little did I know that my life would be changed forever. My hand stopped at Colossians. "You haven't ever taught Colossians," I said to myself. "Maybe this could be the solution to stagnation."

I began to read Paul's words to this young church at Colossae. Even from the dark, wet, and cold prison cell of Rome, Paul had such a powerful message to bring. He began his letter in the similar way he addressed the other churches of the New Testament.

Being a man of character, he couldn't forget to remind his fellow brothers and sisters that he constantly remembered all the saints in his prayers, and Colossae wasn't an exception. The relationship they shared was held by a bond stronger than any force known to man, the bond of Jesus Christ.

He quickly moved from thanksgiving to encouragement as he reminded these young Christians about the greatness of God's grace and distinctive truth. He reminded them that through the Son, Jesus Christ, God had rescued their souls from the dominion of darkness and brought them into the kingdom of light.

And then, there it was. Words I had never seen. Scriptures I had never translated. Thoughts I had never considered. With all inspiration and authority, Paul laid it out on the table.

> He is the image of the invisible God, the firstborn over all creation. For by him all things were created: things in heaven and on earth, visible and invisible, whether thrones or powers or rulers or authorities; all things were created by him and for him. He is before all things, and in him all things are held together. (Colossians 1:15–17, NIV)

Wow! What meaning! What purpose! The same Christ who was crucified for my transgressions was, and is, the image of the invisible God.

Like most ministers who *claim* to be analytics, questions and thoughts flooded my mind. I couldn't fathom the real purpose of these verses.

How could Christ be the image of something that was invisible?

Was Paul mistaken? Was this an oxymoron?

How could Christ portray the portrait of something we can't see?

Plus, Paul said that Christ created *all* things (heaven, earth, things that are visible and invisible, thrones, powers, and authorities). But not only did Christ create *all* things but *all* things were created *for* him?

How was that possible? What was the purpose?

Paul's perplexing words not only got my attention but left me wanting more. Surely there was an explanation, and maybe this explanation was the explanation I needed to solve my slump.

I wanted to feel the pinnacle of passion. I wanted to preach the word of the Lord with boldness once again, but I needed that extra push. If only I could understand why Paul penned these priceless, ancient words.

As I continued to read, Paul's next sentence gave me every reason to continue my search for meaning.

Not only was Christ the image of the invisible God who created *all* things and for whom *all* things were created, but he was also the head of the church.

Now, this I knew. It was common vocabulary. It had been ingrained in my mind since I was a small boy, but it still gave me a reality check.

I was a minister, Christ's servant, with the amazing yet humbling task to tell his story to the world. I had given my life to the church, and this Christ who was the head was also the image of the invisible.

I couldn't turn back. With every inkling of my body, I had to digest and grasp this life changing description of Jesus Christ.

But as I stared at those empty sermon ideas, that were beginning to materialize, I was reminded of one of the first rules of Bible study. To fully digest the message, we have to place the "text in context." We have to form the bridge from that ancient world to our contemporary lives.

When Paul wrote these powerful words, he was obviously addressing his family of believers at Colossae, but below the surface, behind the ink, and beyond the discussions of church committees and coffee shops, there was another group that Paul had in mind, the Gnostics.

The Gnostics weren't pioneer Republicans. They weren't innovative, radical Democrats. They were their own Libertarians of the day.

They didn't argue for the physical, political welfare of all people. Their minds focused on spiritual things that were anything but the true spirit of Christ.

Their name derived from the Greek word "knowsis," meaning knowledge. In their own arrogant, yet tragic way, they truly believed their intellectual abilities paved a crooked, untravelled road to salvation. And better yet? Only *they* could understand this "wisdom."

The Gnostics' platform was shaky at best. One could say their arguments were as stable as the "straw man." Any spiritually informed individual, who desired a deeper understanding of God, could challenge their theology.

The Gnostics claimed that God was good and pure because he was a Spirit. Any physical matter—the earth, the human body, the food we eat, the clothes we wear, the houses we build, they're all evil because they don't have "spirit-like" qualities.

So if God is good because God is Spirit, how could his Son Jesus, be God, since Jesus was composed of evil matter?

This was impossible. This defied all laws of Gnostic thinking. Therefore, since this Christian theory didn't fit the Gnostics "bill," Jesus was a crock.

He wasn't a good God. Jesus was an evil human, a sorely mistaken leader, and a desperate liar.

Paul knew these maniacs were infecting the early church. Not only were they well known, but they were very influential, and they could bust up a church like an earthquake. It was only a matter of time before the Gnostics devoured Colossae.

Paul spoke up because he knew something had to be done. God is always good, and earth exists because of the good and perfect gifts, and not only is God always good, but his Son is perfect.

So Paul made it painfully clear: "He is the image of the invisible God!"

He is the blueprint of Almighty God enthroned in heavenly glory we cannot see but dream to experience. He is God in the flesh, and he dwells among men!

Once again, Paul pulled on the chords of my heart. Just like the Gnostics, I had ignored the power of Jesus

Christ. He was my passion. He was my purpose. He was the one I couldn't touch, but the one I could always find. And if this Jesus could turn my life upside down, he must have influenced these critics of the cosmos. After all, he is the image of the invisible God.

And then, like a ton of bricks, it hit every bone in my body. Perplexing Paul was no longer "perplexing." It all made sense. Did he write these words for the church at Colossae?

That's obvious. Did he preach the words against the Gnostic posse? Absolutely.

But most of all, with his inspired hand, Paul wrote these words for people like me.

People like you.

People who need to be reminded, "You serve a purpose. You have a plan. You make the difference."

Not only was Christ the image of the invisible God.

1. But as a child of God created in that same image, *I've* been given the responsibility to be the image of the invisible God.
2. As a child of God created in that same image, *you've* been given the responsibility to illustrate the image of the invisible God.

Let's take a journey to see how.

Discussion Questions:

1) When you hear the words, "Image of the Invisible God," what image comes to your mind?

_____

_____

_____

2) Have you ever felt "burnout" in your life? If so, when and why?

_____

_____

_____

3) How will the framework for this book, Colossians 1:15-17, push you to be better as you continue to read?

_____

_____

_____

Chapter Two

What is Jesus's Image?

A s we read through the Gospels that so simply, yet eloquently illustrate Jesus's life, we form a faint image in our minds of Jesus from Nazareth.

He was an ambitious preteen who challenged scholars in the temple courts. As a carpenter's son, he was most likely in tip top physical condition with muscle definition.

I'm sure his hands were torn from the stress of labor. His feet weary from the roads less traveled. His eyes full of compassion for the sick and distressed. His heart aching for perishing souls.

But even though this was the "alleged" appearance of God in the flesh, the Messiah didn't stand out in the crowd. The paparazzi wouldn't struggle to flash snippets of his life.

In fact, even the prophet Isaiah, prophesied about Jesus's aura in this unique way, "He had not beauty or majesty to attract us to him, nothing in his appearance that we should desire him" (Isaiah 53: 2, NIV). That's right. From the outside looking in, the man who would change history was the "Average Joe."

But even though Christ's physical image didn't grab the attention of every eye, his *spiritual* image is remembered forever.

His legacy echoes from the lonely hill of Golgotha. Three crosses of death stood near the sunset of life but only the cross in the middle held any significance. It was a chapter that ended in human defeat, but a novel that continues in God's victory.

And this is the life, the calling, the torch that we are to carry. Just like Jesus, we are the image of the invisible God. So what exactly does that image portray?

In some theological, miraculous, and divine way that our human minds can't fully understand, Jesus and God the Father are one. Sure, God is enthroned in heaven, and he always has been, and Jesus is sitting at God's right hand, but even though Jesus came to earth and separated himself from the heavenly realms for three decades, they were still one.

There are some seventy-two different ways that the Bible describes God. Some descriptions are Hebrew, some are Aramaic, and some are Greek, but they all describe God in different ways.

Jesus also has different names which give us a special glimpse into this character. They compose the image we should reflect because these names visualize that which is invisible.

Christ

Christ is the most common way that Jesus is remembered. It almost seems like it is Jesus's last name. Even when people speak out of turn and take the Lord's name in vain, they can't just say "Jesus" in their disgust, they must complete their connotation with "Christ."

But have you ever considered what "Christ" means, the counterpart of Jesus's memory?

We can form a faint definition for "Christ" by relying on the Hebrew and Greek languages. Both languages give definitions that differ in linguistic wording, but they create the same theological image. In Hebrew, "Christ" means "Messiah." In Greek, "Christ" means "Anointed One."

It was custom in the Old Testament and ancient world to anoint leaders with oil. Kings didn't receive crowns as they were lifted to the throne; a leader of the kingdom would come and anoint their head with oil to show the nation's confidence and respect in their new king. This anointing was both honorable and symbolic.

It was honorable in the sense that no other man in the land was receiving this type of therapeutic service, but it was also symbolic in the sense that this man had been chosen by the people to be their hero.

Being chosen is a common part of life. When we're chosen for an athletic team, we're chosen because the captain thinks we can compete. When we're chosen for a job, we're chosen because an employer hopes we will produce. When we're chosen by our spouse, we're chosen because our helper believes we're loveable and worthy. Regardless if we volunteer or we're picked off a whim, we have a task.

Jesus the "Christ" knew he was chosen for a reason. It wasn't a task that was popular or envied. For many, it wasn't even a task that made sense. It was a job that was necessary to change history and reconcile billions of souls back to their creator—*something only he could do.*

How do we feel about the "Christ," the "Anointed One" who was chosen for this purpose?

We say we remember him, but he quickly fades away in discussions of politics, money, sex, and fame. We might say the cross stands at the center of our life, but the cross gets pushed aside by the desires of wealth and pleasure.

But we don't have a choice. We have to remember him. We have to see the crystal clarity of his purpose. This image of God, which is so rampantly becoming invisible in our world, brings us back to the same picture of Jesus.

He is the "Christ." He was picked by the pride of God. He was anointed with all power, wisdom, truth, and understanding. He was punished for the sin of the world—even the sin of those who would reject him in his time of greatest need.

He was chosen.
Chosen for you.
Chosen for me.

Lord

It's impossible to see Christ's image without focusing on his Lordship. The chosen apostles, the strangers on the street, even the Pharisees in deceit, referred to Jesus as "Lord." In the ancient world, the term "lord" was as common as "sir."

Everyone had a "lord" in their life. Slaves had a lord in their masters, children had a lord in their parents, wives had a lord in their husbands, and citizens had a lord in their government.

But "lord" is a basic term that's often misunderstood. "Lord" simply means "master." It's the emotional and verbal understanding that "I, as your subordinate, will do as you say."

This concept of authority has always been embedded into the wrinkles of the human mind. Even in the garden, Adam knew that he was in subjection to God and the Tree of Knowledge of Good and Evil. He was to honor God's instruction and fear the tree's doom.

As humans, we must answer to authority, regardless if the "commander" is mortal or immortal.

But when Christ's image is portrayed as the "Lord" of our lives, we must obey with sincerity. Jesus will control our thoughts, our actions, our victories, our defeats, and our purpose. Unfortunately, we don't always focus on this spectacle of the Savior's image.

Wouldn't it have been life changing to hear Jesus's plea for authority? The man with all authority in heaven and on earth, pleading with his personal followers to give credit to whom credit was due? But one of the most painful, if not embarrassing things to hear, was when Jesus looked at those twelve chosen men we call the "apostles" and asked them, "Why do you call me Lord, and not do what I tell you to do?" (Luke 6:46, NIV)

Yes, that's right. Why do you call me your master and respond through the stubbornness of your life, "No, sir, I will not do as you say."

What a blow! What a reality check! What an opportunity to say, "It's time to get real." I have made this Jesus and Christ, the Lord of my life, but I have no interest in mimicking my master?

When Jesus poses such a tragic question, we don't have the luxury to ignore his candid curiosity. Why do we call Jesus our Lord, but then neglect to do what he tells us to do?

Just like many problems in life, there isn't one answer. There are a variety of reasons floating from mind to mind, heart to heart, and household to household, but nevertheless, successfully and ultimately creating the problem.

We may not obey our master because we lack *commitment*. Our psyches and personalities are interested in doing other things. We live on this earth for a short time, and as the clock continues to tick, our desires take precedent. Life is too short to say no, so we believe that if we want to live life to the fullest, "yes" should be the first word that rolls off our tongue.

We may not obey our Lord because we lack *support*. At times, it feels like we're fighting this battle on our own. Just like Elijah in the cave, we fall to the ground, and we cry out to God, "I'm the only one left!" We convince ourselves that we're the only faithful souls walking the streets of this dark and dreadful world. As a result, in our sense of isolation and despair, we give up because our sense of community has disappeared.

We may not obey our Lord because we lack *faith*. It is human nature, especially in American tradition, to ask, "What will this do for me? Are the rewards worth the struggle?"

Pragmatic evaluation might have a place in American culture, but pragmatism has no place in the Christian's life. We don't follow in the steps of Jesus because of the dividend and return. We listen to his words and captivate on his commands because he is the "Lord" of our lives.

You see, we can give excuses and answer the question with reasonable doubt. We can say we don't buy into

Jesus being "lord" because we lack commitment, support, faith, or any other critical component for Christian success.

However, we can't say we fail to make Jesus the Lord of our life because we lack knowledge! Jesus tells us exactly what he wants. His recipe is clear and easy to follow. Words like "sacrifice," "humility," "dedication," "love," and "obedience" still ring from the streets of Jerusalem and the shores of Galilee. We can see who *we* should be, because we can see who *Jesus* is. Not only is Jesus the chosen one (Christ), but he's also the "master."

Why? He's our Lord. And when we truly see this shadow of his image, we can't say no.

Holy One

In our prayers, we pray to the Holy One. In our songs, we praise the holy Christ and Lord, Jesus Christ. We know who the Holy One is, but what does Holy One mean?

"Holy" means to be "set apart," to be *light* rather than dark, to be *hot* rather than cold, to be *pure* rather than polluted. So if Jesus is the Holy One, he should be different than everything and everyone.

It's true. When we look at his life, Jesus was anything but "ordinary." Every thought, every action, every word was unique.

When people saw Jesus, they saw an "alien" living in a strange land—a pioneer travelling a journey, a pilgrim longing for home.

As a twelve-year-old, he sat in the temple courts discussing spiritual matters with the spiritual experts. As a young adult, he spent his time healing the sick rather than honoring the healthy, helping the poor rather than rewarding the rich, setting an example rather than seeking the status quo. Yes, in everything, Jesus was "set apart." He truly was holy.

However, there's a serious problem. Christ is still set apart in our current world, but not as the Holy One. He's set apart as a "hanus fable."

We have taken God's name out of our schools, and in so doing, we have set apart God and Jesus from our democratic dreams. We are no longer one nation under God but one nation searching for purpose.

It comes as no surprise that as we continue to set apart God from our lives, we become more and more set apart from success.

While he was reasoning with the Athenian government, Paul told the leaders that in God, "we live and move and have our being" (Acts 17:18, NIV). Wouldn't it have been amazing to have stood in that hallowed hall and seen the expressions of those pagan leaders? To see their faces of disgust when they heard, "You live and move and exist because of a God not made by human hands, but rather a God that made you with his"?

Paul wasn't very well received, but Paul got it right. Just like the Athenian government, we have it wrong. We don't live by our hands; every breath of our lungs and beat of our hearts are produced by God.

Our nation continues to crumble and we ask why. We consult all the experts to give us the answer, but these experts don't produce expertise. Sure, they come up with glamorous, band aid solutions that momentarily stop the bleeding, but when they've served their purpose, they're painfully pulled back, and we're opened to infection.

We may choose to be set apart *from* Christ, but he still longs for relationship. He still demands commitment. He still desires transparency.

You see, that image of Christ transcends from Calvary's cross to our door. It's up to us to open the door and invite it in. Not just for coffee, not just for dinner, to stay.

Bread of Life

The "Bread of Life" could be the most unique description of Jesus. It's actually a description Jesus gave himself.

Shortly after Jesus defied all laws of nature and walked on water, Jesus began his next tutorial. Even though the disciples had just seen a miraculous event, like spoiled children, they still weren't satisfied with their circumstances.

In their unbelievable immaturity, all they could focus on was their next meal. Jesus gave them the cure to their cravings. He looked into their broken lives and said, "I am the bread of life. He who comes to me will never go hungry" (John 6:35, NIV).

Excuse me? *You*, the man we're watching and following, you're the cuisine? You're the bread? How could this be?

It would have been crazy to hear that hunger could be filled through flesh. Obviously, Jesus was not referring to a *physical* loaf of bread. He was the *substance, the nourishment, the food that would sustain their lives!*

When we look at the origination of this term, it tells a fabulous story and builds a powerful connection. When Jesus was born, he didn't enter the world as royalty. There wasn't any pomp and circumstance—only unknown visitors who travelled to Bethlehem bringing simple gifts to a child born in a manger.

Roughly translated from the Hebrew, Bethlehem means "house of bread." Many cities in the ancient world held significant meanings. Jerusalem was known as the city of David and for a good reason, it was one of David's most prized possessions. He was the founder and patriarch of the city, which would ironically, crucify Jesus, also known as the "son of David."

But why was Bethlehem named the house of bread?

In the Old Testament, we read a fabulous love story in the book of Ruth.

Ruth followed her mother-in-law Naomi to the city of Bethlehem after her husband, Naomi's son, had passed away. On arriving in Bethlehem, Ruth worked hard gleaning all of the grain in the fields. Around the clock, she worked with diligence and worked harder than any man.

This grabbed the attention of Boaz, one of the great leaders of the town of Bethlehem. Boaz decided to do his "research" on Ruth to learn more about this new beautiful icon of Bethlehem.

Boaz learned about her faithfulness to her mother-in-law, Naomi. He saw her spirit of hard work and godly nobility. They fell in love, and Ruth once again entered into the joys of marriage with Boaz.

Here's the connection: Bethlehem, the house of bread, stored all of the bread for the ancient world. When people were hungry, they travelled to Bethlehem. When people were struggling, they depended on Bethlehem. When people needed stability, they longed for Bethlehem. Bethlehem was the only place they could find food, and it was the source of the world's survival.

Do we see any connections with Christ? He's the house of bread. He's the bread that gives us life. He's the *only* source for the world's survival.

When we're hungry, we need the bread. When we're struggling, we need the Christ. When we're lost, we need to be found by the Savior. When was the last time you yearned for the bread of life?

We pursue so many "snacks" or "meals" that we *believe* will provide us with everything we need. With earthly food, hunger ceases for a while, but before we know it, we're hungry again. But with Christ, whenever we hunger for him, we're always filled.

Jesus says, "Come to me. I will give you fulfillment.

Come to me, you will never hunger again.

Come to me, I am the bread of life. Come to me, you will never look back."

Why don't you listen? Why don't you come? The Bread of Life is waiting for you.

Prince of Peace

Smoke fills the sky. Bombs blast buildings. Nations fight nations. People always die. It's the unfortunate, yet unavoidable consequences of war.

For thousands of years, inhabitants of the world have been encouraged or, some cases, brainwashed, to defend that which they believe is worth defending. That's why it comes as no surprise when Jesus told Peter, James, Andrew, and John on the Mount of Olives overlooking Jerusalem, "Nation will rise against nation, and kingdom against kingdom" (Mark 13:8, NIV)

Since that day, we've seen nations and kingdoms take the lives and legacies of their enemies. As soon as one life is created, another one is demolished. It's the cycle of the human struggle for power.

Today, nations don't rise against nations because of God's providential militant charge. Nations fight nations because of zealous and often evil desires for control.

As a full-time minister, I often hear prayers from some of the godliest men I know pleading for God to provide peace. The flashbacks of yesteryear fill their memories and hearts with pain of war. They can still smell the gun smoke, they can still hear the cries of fear, and they can still see the blood of their countrymen flowing to the ground, as hot lead poured through their bodies.

Why? A nation commanded them to fight, so they grabbed the rifle and stood on the wall in the spirit of honor. Now, years later, as they remember the horrific events of their past, they beg God to shelter this generation and the generations to come from the tragedies of war.

Should we pray for peace? Will the prayers provide what we're looking for?

Prayer is certainly encouraged and needed. Jesus once said,

> Ask and it will be given to you; seek and you
> will find; knock and the door will be opened
> to you. For everyone who asks receives; he who
> seeks finds; and to him who knocks, the door
> will be opened. (Matthew 7: 7–8, NIV)

Approaching God in prayer and asking him to
provide peace is a reasonable approach. Jesus even says
that by asking, we will find. Certainly, peace would be
reachable through prayer.

I just wonder if peace can be found through other
venues. Instead of praying through Jesus's name asking
for peace, why not *look* to Jesus as the example? Instead
of searching for harmony, why not *find* Jesus?

It was the prophet Isaiah who spoke of Jesus's
peaceful credentials. As he was prophesying about this
child who would be born, this child who would change
the world forever through dignity and majesty, Isaiah
also said that this omnipotent being would serve as our
"Prince of Prince" (Isaiah 9:6, NIV).

What a tremendous title, what a powerful tag line.
The prince of tranquility, serenity, and eternity.

We've been told, and conditioned to believe, that
peace can only be found through chaotic and violent
measures. If we want peace, we have to fight. If we want
peace, we have to die. If we want peace, we must protect
a nation that won't always protect us.

Isn't this ironic? As we strive for peace, we succumb to chaos? As we yearn for safety, we welcome danger?

But Jesus has a different strategy.

He says, "Come to me, and you will find peace. Follow me, and I will calm your life like I calmed the seas."

Following Christ isn't easy. Discipleship comes with a cost. But at the end of the day, after we've run our race, we feel the peace our prince provides.

And what's so special about Jesus being the Prince of Peace is that Jesus provides peace with *authority*. He isn't the servant of peace. He isn't even the agent of peace. He's the prince of the virtue for which men give their lives.

War will continue to devastate countries. From ocean to ocean, innocent people will continue to die. From continent to continent, nation will continue to rise against nation.

Through prayer, we can approach the throne of God with confidence and pray for peace and good will toward all men. But let's remember, prayer isn't our only hope or option. We have Jesus, the Prince of Peace.

Counselor

We've all been there. We've all experienced that sense of isolation, where we long for someone to understand the feelings that wear on our soul.

When these feelings darken our door, we immediately search for trained professionals to come to the rescue. Regardless if it's a psychiatrist, psychologist, or a minister, we're looking for a counselor.

Jesus is willing to serve in this capacity. In fact, Jesus puts the offer on the table.

Isaiah referred to him this way, when Isaiah wrote, "For to us a child is born, to us a son is given, and the government will be on his shoulders. And he will be called Wonderful Counselor" (Isaiah 9:6, NIV).

When we're looking for that special source of wisdom to guide us through the jungles of life, what qualities do we desire in a counselor?

If you're anything like me, you probably want a counselor who understands your struggles. You don't want to open up your heart to someone who can't relate. You might desire a counselor who is fair and will speak in your defense to your superiors or oppressors. To find comfort, you don't want to be criticized or rejected.

You might long for a counselor who can actually offer the advice that leads to solutions. What good is a counselor if they can't actually counsel?

If we're true to ourselves and appropriately respectful toward Christ, he fulfills all of these wants and needs.

Jesus can sympathize with the struggles we endure. Regardless if it's temptation, sadness, jealousy, or disappointment, He's been there. He can relate.

The Hebrew writer described Jesus's similarities with these words,

> For we do not have a high priest who is unable to sympathize with our weaknesses, but we have one who has been tempted in every way, just as we are—yet was without sin. Let us then approach the throne of grace with confidence, so that we may receive mercy and find grace to help us in our time of need.
>
> (Hebrews 4:15–16, NIV).

Why wouldn't you seek counsel from a man like that? A man who can talk the talk and walk the walk because he's walked a mile in your shoes. With his past, he can solve your present.

And unlike any other counselor, Jesus will help us on the most important day of our existence, the Day of Judgment. Every knee will bow and every tongue will finally confess that Jesus is Lord. We won't have any doubt what's taking place because we will hear the trumpets sound and see the Lord descend on a cloud of glory as we meet him in the air.

When that day comes, we will want security. Good news. We will find that security in our counselor.

Paul wrote to the young preacher Timothy and said, "For there is one God and one mediator between God and men, the man Christ Jesus, who gave himself as a ransom for all men" (1 Timothy 2:5–6, NIV).

As a mediator and counselor, Christ will defend us before God. When God judges what we've done or haven't done, if we have lived lives worthy of our calling, Christ will speak up and say, "He's on our team. She's with us. Welcome home."

Will Jesus know our weaknesses, struggles, and faults? Of course. He knows everything about us.

But he loves us so much that he supports us and speaks in our defense because he knows just what we need—eternity with him.

And without a doubt, as our counselor, Christ will always support us. He's in the business of helping people—"a man who did not come to be served, but to serve, and give His life as a ransom for many" (Matthew 20:28, NIV).

Jesus was speaking and listening to his disciples, searching into their hearts and seeking their inner most thoughts, because he wanted to be the solution. After hearing about their struggles and concerns, Jesus said, "Come to me, all you who are weary and burdened, and I will give you rest" (Matthew 11:28, NIV). In other words, "I'm here for you. I'm here to help you. Not only do I want your life to be enjoyable, I want to make it wonderful."

Can we find that magnitude of support in any other counselor? Sure, some counselors might strive to help improve our lives, but even in their most dedicated theories, they can never compare with the counsel of Christ.

When Jesus promises that life is in him, and everything we need comes from his hand, he means it. He's our purpose, our life, our all.

The question is—will you let him counsel you?

Redeemer

"Hold on to your ticket, and wait for the next available agent. They will redeem your coupon at the desk." Do these words sound familiar? Have you ever waited hours to redeem something you didn't need? Sure you have.

Ten percent off your next purchase of peanuts. Forty percent of that swimsuit for the Christmas season. A "buy one, get one free" ping pong set.

Excellent work! These items will certainly come in handy. And good for you for saving money.

We're always looking for something or someone to "redeem" us. During the last few years of economic crisis, we've all felt the pressure of pinching pennies. Homes have been refinanced. Luxury cars have been traded in for more practical transportation. Some have even cut their losses and given up their mortgages all together in search for the simpler life.

When these money struggles surface, we immediately desire redemption. Who can give us some grace? Who can change our interest rate? Who can open up some cash flow? We need a redeemer—someone to say, "You're slate has been wiped clean."

But we seek redemption beyond the check book ledger. Our relationships are broken. Our hearts are scattered into a million pieces because we haven't been the husband, wife, father, or mother we were supposed to be.

Can't we get another chance? Aren't there any do-overs? Will we ever be able to replace the years of heartache that we've lost?

Or we travel down this street of sorrow. "By now, I was supposed to be a _____." Or "At this age, I was supposed to have _____ number of dollars in savings."

Has it happened? Are you the _____ you thought you would be? Do you have _____ number of dollars providing a competitive return? Probably not. Life doesn't always turn out like we think it will.

But there's still that thought in the back of our minds, "I can do this. If only someone would redeem my failures, I could be who I was supposed to be. I could do what I was supposed to do."

We all need a redeemer. But we have a redeemer, if we choose to accept the redemption.

This redeemer went to the cross to redeem us of sin. He gave his life on the tree to redeem our shortcomings, so that when the world sees defeat, God sees victory. God calls us his own because his one and only Son Jesus, our Redeemer, made it possible.

But Jesus's redemption also travels beyond our *sin*. Jesus heals our broken relationships. Jesus provides the forgiveness, we, in turn, are commanded to provide others. Jesus models true friendship. Jesus helps us achieve forsaken goals.

When we feel like we can't, Jesus says we can. When we fall to our feet, Jesus causes us to stand. As his power flows through our body, he molds us into who he wants us to be.

Our past is redeemed by transforming our future.

You see, Jesus wants nothing more than to redeem us from our troubles. Regardless if it's sin that leads to death, families that struggle to survive, or goals that define character, Jesus redeems it all.

Job was one of the most godly, faithful men to ever live. Satan tested Job by taking his family, finances, and favor, but Job remained faithful to God and stood the test of faith.

And even during his toughest hours, Job found comfort in heavenly redemption. With confidence Job said, "I know that my Redeemer lives, and that in the end he will stand upon the earth." (Job 19:25, NIV)

If you haven't noticed, Job was right.

Immanuel

Have you ever watched young parents agonize over the names to choose for their children? They want to choose names that bring power and honor to the family legacy, names that describe their children perfectly.

Can you blame them? It took four months for my wife and me to choose the name for our first child, Hayden Jacob Hawk.

Isn't it interesting that Judas isn't common for boys and Jezebel isn't common for girls? What parent in their right mind would name their precious little boy after the greedy scoundrel who betrayed Jesus for thirty measly pieces of silver? How could a father or mother look at their gorgeous little girl and say, "You look like a Jezebel"? Jezebel? She was only one of the most evil women to ever walk the earth, but Jezebel has a nice ring to it!

It doesn't happen. Names begin our destiny.

It reminds me of the young man who was about to graduate college, but he only had one class left to take, bird watching.

He studied birds the entire semester. Their eating routines. Their bone structures. Their preferred habitats. He even woke up early in the morning to watch them in the trees.

It finally came time for that final exam, and he studied all night for the last test. He got up the next morning with confidence, but when the professor passed out the exam, there was a serious problem.

The entire test was pictures of bird legs. That's it. Bird legs. They were supposed to look at these legs and give the name of the birds just by looking at their legs.

That young man stood up, threw his test down, walked over to the professor's desk and said, "This is ridiculous. You're crazy. This entire semester has been a waste of time, and you have stolen four months of my life. I'm out of here!"

He turned away in frustration to walk out the door. Right as he was about to leave, the professor said, "Young man, what is your name?" That cocky college student didn't miss a beat but reached down, grabbed his pant leg, pulled up it past his knee, and said, "You tell me!"

God chose his son's name very carefully. Jesus was going to be the perfector of God's plan. Someone that important needed a name that adequately described his greatness. Thomas, Peter, even Bartholomew, were catchy names, but they didn't make the cut. Jesus needed a "tagline" that would set him apart for history.

Jesus's name was common, but it wasn't the most popular of his day. Even today, it still doesn't make the list of common names for children.

However, his name is in a league of its own. His name makes life worth living.

When Jesus entered the world, he entered in a time of confusion. He was born to a virgin mother, and Joseph, the father and very righteous man, wasn't really sure how to handle the situation. He even considered divorcing Mary because of her probable infidelity. He hadn't had sexual relations with her, so she must have conceived this child with another man.

An angel calmed Joseph's and Mary's nerves and also relieved the pressure of naming this new gift from God. They would name him Jesus, because he "would save his people from their sins," but Jesus would be remembered by a different name, Immanuel, because "God is with us."

There couldn't be a better name. Jesus is with us everywhere we go. It is impossible to enter a place where Jesus can't follow us.

Jesus is in our *homes*, or at least, he should be! The American moral compass is more lost than it has ever been. It seems like every year we fall further and further from the people Jesus wants us to be but, there is hope. Jesus can help us achieve Christian homes because Jesus wants to be a part of the home. Jesus wants to be a member of the family. We just have to include him in our rooms and at our tables.

Jesus is at our *jobs*. He might get pushed to the side under last week's paperwork or left on the stove with yesterday's coffee, but Jesus is still there. He's ready to show us the ways to go and the steps to take. He wants to be active and relevant to the work place. The problem is, the workers don't always wish for him to be there.

Jesus is in our *lives*. He's ready to smile in times of victory. He's ready to hold us in times of defeat. He's there when we decide who we want to be and what we want to become. He's there when we set our financial, physical, and spiritual goals. He wants to help, and with his help, he makes our lives whole.

You see, Jesus has always been with us, he's with us today, and he will be with us for eternity. Do *you* choose to see *him*? Take a look. Open your eyes. You'll like what you see.

Savior

We all long for a savior. It doesn't matter how old we are; we still desire that hero to captivate our life and lead us down the path of security.

Regardless if we're a leader or a follower, we aren't capable to provide our own refuge. There have been many times in my life when I've desperately needed that knight in shining armor.

I remember it just like it was yesterday. Living in Dallas, my family and I often went to watch the Texas Rangers during the summer. However, on this particular day, as we pulled up to Ranger's Stadium, an overwhelming feeling of independence controlled my mind—a very dangerous thing for a little boy.

As soon as we walked through the gates, it was my time to shine. I wanted my own peanuts, my own cotton candy, my own program, my own ice cream. Isn't it interesting I didn't want to buy my own ticket?

Anyway, during the seventh inning stretch, I realized it was time for the bathroom. It was my own bladder, so it might as well have been my own trip to the men's room. There I was, an independent boy on a passionate quest for urinary liberation.

Finding the bathroom wasn't too much of a challenge. As soon as I walked through the tunnel that led to our seats, the bathroom was immediately on the left. I walked in, did my business, and everything was going as planned. Proud of my "manly" accomplishment, I then embarked on the next leg of my journey, finding my seat.

Problem! Big problem! Which way do I go?

Which section are the seats?

Which row?

Where's my ticket?

All of these panicked questions without answers. I could feel the hair standing up on the back of my neck and my eyes filling with tears.

I ran out into the crowded area that passed in front of snack stands, crying at the top of my lungs, "*Mom! Dad! Where are you?*"

It wasn't supposed to happen this way. This was my day to grow up and become a man, but here I was lost in the world of overpriced pretzels and nachos.

And then it happened. My savior walked toward me with arms wide open. She was an older lady with the sweet disposition of a grandmother. Her cheeks were rosy, her eyes were full of love, and her heart as good as gold.

She asked me, "Sweetheart, can I help you?" It didn't take her long to figure out how she could save the day.

She helped me find my ticket, which by this time had been buried underneath peanut shells in my pocket. (Who cares about the peanuts? The fun is cracking the shells and keeping them for later!) She read my ticket, grabbed my hand, and led me to my parents. Without a doubt, she was my savior.

Even if we aren't that boy walking through the valley of the shadow of death called the men's restroom, we've all found ourselves in the same hole of desperation. We realize that we don't know where to go. We can't figure out our next move. We feel hopeless because we need a savior.

It sounds strange, but at times, we need to be saved from our *families*. Even with those we love the most, tension can build to the point of breaking bonds. Those we're supposed to cherish, we condemn. Those we're supposed to protect, we persecute. "Family" is nothing more than built up feelings of regret. We need that hero to save our family.

At times we need to be saved from our *friends*. We thought they would always look out for us. We thought we could always confide in their confidentiality. But unfortunately, we can't. They aren't who we thought they were. Not only have they hurt our feelings, they've destroyed our reputation. The last thing we need is another get together or coffee date. We need a genius to save the relationship.

Every day as we turn on the news, it becomes so clear that we need to be saved from the *world*. Nation after nation falls to the dark and dreadful depths of civil war. Business after business files bankruptcy. This world isn't a place we belong, much less a place where we want to be. The only light at the end of the tunnel is the saving image of the ever after.

Granted, we all differ in our views of family, friends, and this world. Some of us have favorable memories and perceptions, while some of us feel the sting of yesterday and the disappointment of today. *However*, we all need to be saved from one thing, sin. Sin separates us from God. Sin controls our lives. Sin defines who we are and where we will spend eternity.

Thankfully, Jesus is the solution. Our loving Savior gave his life to cure us from the worldwide epidemic.

Jesus said, "For God so loved the world, that He gave His one and only son, that whoever believes in Him shall not perish, but have eternal life" (John 3:16, NIV).

That's a pretty high view of self, but that view is reality. When Jesus spoke those words, he meant it. He knew his role. He was, is, and always will be, the Savior.

When you long for a Savior, Jesus answers the call because he's ready to save your life. Let him.

Christ, Lord, Holy One, Bread of Life, Prince of Peace, Counselor, Redeemer, Immanuel, and Savior. Not every name, but several names that describe Jesus. Names that perfectly illustrate his image the world claims is invisible.

But *we* see who he is and who *we* need to be.

Is this the image(s) you portray? The world tells us we're supposed to appear much differently, and if I were to guess, you've been affected!

Let's see how.

Discussion Questions:

1) Which description of Jesus do you find most captivating?

_____

_____

_____

2) Which description of Jesus do you find most challenging?

_____

_____

_____

3) Which description of Jesus do you appreciate the most, and why?

_____

_____

_____

Chapter Three

The World's Image?

A s we've seen so far, there's no shortage of illustrations for Jesus's image. From his Lordship to his servant hood, the image of Jesus Christ is a milestone we must strive to reach. How can we go wrong imitating the Son of God, the true statute of perfection?

Unfortunately, it's impossible for us to ignore the world's handcuffs that handicap our potential.

Jesus shows us who we *need* to be, but the world manipulates us into what they say we *should* be. When Jesus preaches holiness, the world preaches conformity. When Jesus exemplifies faithfulness, the world exemplifies infidelity. When Jesus promotes peace, the world promotes violence.

We can't prevent the world from being the world, but we can control how influential the world will be in our lives.

For us to truly reflect Christ, we must understand the image the *world* wants us to reflect. If we aren't aware of the world's message, we will quickly fall victim to its teachings, and when that happens, we're dead men walking.

So *who* or *what* image does the world tell us to portray?

Pull off the Pounds

You're placing the ice cream, donuts, chips, and sodas on the counter in the checkout line, and you can't wait to get home and gorge yourself with some of life's simplest pleasures. But then, it happens.

As you're watching your favorite treats travel into those plastic bags, you see the monument that has purposely been erected before your eyes—a gorgeous, handsome, sexy model, with stomach muscles only computers can create, staring a hole of guilt right through your chest.

Those models have been plastered on those overpriced magazines for one reason—*to convince you it's time to turn your life around by falling victim to the latest diet fad.*

It's a simple message really. We're happy. We've got it all figured out. If you can look like us, your problems will disappear. You can get that girl. You can have that guy. The job will be yours. Sex will be even better. Why? Because you can iron that shirt that's already too tight on your washboard abs, and when you put on the shirt that's three sizes too small, your bank account gets bigger and everyone's eyes are immediately drawn to your breathtaking physique.

Okay, maybe I'm being a little sarcastic and blowing it out of proportion. But then again, I don't think I'm too far from reality. Our society obsesses over being thin.

Every week, these magazines come out with new diet ideas.

Take this pill. Drink this solution. Eat this ingredient. If you do, you will lose thirty pounds in thirty days. Or my personal favorite is when magazines printed in July advertise, "There's still time to get into that summer bikini!"

Still time? Maybe if you live in the Sahara Desert and your favorite Christmas sweater is sandals and a swimsuit.

It's ridiculous to believe that we can lose thirty, forty, or fifty pounds in just a few weeks. Unfortunately, we believe it. We read the magazines, we buy the pills, we drink the solutions, and we swallow the ingredients, all because society promises it works.

Many Americans exercise, but even more Americans are obese.

What does that tell us? People exercise because the world influences their thinking, but ironically, the world's pressure for exercise doesn't change people's struggle with weight.

You get the point. The world doesn't have the answers. The world will never admit it, but it's true.

There are many factors that can lead to obesity. What about depression? What about food addictions? The treadmill and dumbbells are only simple suggestions, but there's so much more beneath the surface the world doesn't mention or, in some cases, even consider.

Now, it's obviously a good idea to exercise, and we need to exercise as often as we possibly can. I'm not advocating giving up the sweat and sit-ups.

Paul tells us in 1 Corinthians 6 that our bodies are a living temple created by God. Since our physical forms are God's temple, we need to take care of them.

But there's a big difference between healthy exercise and obsession to be a size zero.

Being healthy is important, but that small waist line isn't the solution to our problems, and it can't be the focus of our lives. Unless we Photoshop our bodies, we will always struggle to reflect the image of super models. Regrettably, when society demands unrealistic expectations for our appearance, we listen, and we cave.

Build Up the Bank Account

Money talks. These common words have controlled Americans' values since our nation's inception. The more money in our pockets, the more power we have. When the wealthy speak, people listen, because money has a voice of its own.

It doesn't matter if we live in the north, south, east, or west, the luxurious life style is coveted by American dreamers pursuing the American dream. We want bigger houses, nicer cars, and faster computers. What used to be nice is now mediocre.

It's no longer respectful to prepare for retirement, but now Americans must prepare and compete for the pomp and circumstance of the Jones'.

The days of working for the same company for forty years and building up retirement through loyalty are gone. We constantly wait for the next best deal to come around, and that deal is always defined by the best paycheck. If it benefits us we leave; if it doesn't, we stay, and we wait for something that will.

Why are we so obsessed with our financial image?

Just like we strive to fit in the clothes we can't wear, we strive to build up our bank accounts with money we don't have.

It gets back to the same principle—that's what society has told us to do.

But what about raising a godly family? What about living within your means? What about forming a respectful reputation in your community through acts of service and charity?

Oh, these things are nice, but according to our society, they don't provide true success.

We're only successful if we have the pension, the 401k, the meaningless possessions, and an image that can only be bought by those who can't afford it.

And here's the real kicker: When the business fails, when the economy falls, when the large homes and fancy cars are repossessed, where's society? Do they come to the rescue? Do they still love you unconditionally? Do they still treat you like first class?

No, they simply watch from afar, lose respect, and change perception because you no longer fit into their club. Your money doesn't impress, so consequently, you're no longer worth the time.

Pretty unfair, isn't it?

Don't be surprised. That's the result of listening to the world's lies. Money isn't everything. Money only speaks to those who foolishly listen.

Get that Degree!

We go to college, so we can get our BA. We continue our studies and earn our MBA, and then our Ph.D, so we can be CEO of IBM and drive a BMW.

Yes, the more hours we have in the classroom, the better results we produce. At least that's what the world wants us to believe.

Unfortunately, there's no such thing as a free lunch.

The more degrees we earn, the more debt we incur.

The more debt to our name, the longer it takes to get in the black.

The longer it takes to get in the black, the longer it takes to get ahead.

The longer it takes to get ahead, the longer it takes to retire.

The longer it takes to retire… Well, you get the idea.

Now, degrees are nice. I spent eight years getting mine, and I'm glad that I have them—but those framed, expensive pieces of paper hanging in my office aren't the end to all means. Just like society defines success by pounds and dollars, they also believe that degrees are variables in the unreasonable equation of triumph, and we must listen to the mathematical mystery.

If you have a college degree, ask yourself these questions:

1. *Am I using my degree in my career*?
   Over 50 percent of college graduates enter careers different from their degree training. How does a business degree set you apart from the other thousands of college students studying business? The degree doesn't give the job. The job is received from helpful networking and a solid reputation. Unless you're pursing professions in medicine or law, that degree plan doesn't

mean much. What matters is that you graduate. Degrees don't get jobs. People get jobs.

2. *What did I learn in college?*
   As I just mentioned, most people don't attribute their success to their time in the classroom. If you're in finance, which stocks did you study in western civilization 101? If you're in medicine, what medicine did you find most interesting in art appreciation? If you're in sales, what gifted techniques did you develop in kinesiology? That degree tells employers one thing: I'm a hard worker, and I'll get the job done. It takes commitment to graduate. Intuitive employers know this same commitment will work its way into the workplace.

3. *Would I do it again?*
   I know those college years are cherished by many, but be honest, would you really sign up for another four years? Can't you remember the sleep sacrificed for study? Can't you remember the ramen noodles because the money wasn't there for the $6.95 lunch? Can't you remember the twin-size beds in the dormitory that smelled like gym socks and the thin, moldy walls?

You see, the grass is always greener on the other side. It's like the old farmer who said, "The grass is greener on the other side, but that's because the cows fertilize it more." Good point.

College is important, and it does help us get ahead in life, but at what cost? We always give up something.

If we pursue college, that's our choice, and it's a good one, but we shouldn't enroll just because the world tells us it's necessary. We should pursue higher education because we have the desire.

If we make decisions in life based only on the world's recommendation, we will be sorely disappointed and terribly misguided.

What Has It Got You?

Okay, so you've pulled off the pounds. You've built up that bank account. You've devoted years of your life to the classroom, and you've got that degree.

What has it got you? Does the world view you as a success? Do they throw you parades? Do they admit they can't wait to be like you? Of course they do—every time you walk on water.

Hence, the sarcasm?

It doesn't happen because the world doesn't care. They want you to believe they do, but they don't. And what's even more tragic is that you're competing against *yourself* because you believe they do.

You see, there's only one source that truly cares.

We know him by several different names—Christ, Lord, Holy One, Bread of Life, Prince of Peace, Counselor, Redeemer, Immanuel, and Savior. But if we listen to him, he tells us how to matter—be the "image of the invisible God!"

Discussion Questions:

1) Which one of the world's lies has deceived you the most?

_____

_____

_____

2) When did you realize that you had been deceived?

_____

_____

_____

3) How will you capture the truth, and surrender the deception?

_____

_____

_____

Chapter Four

Changing Your Image

I hope you've enjoyed our journey so far. We're on the quest to discover and define the "image of the invisible God." His image is real, even when the world claims that it's fiction.

We've seen descriptions of Jesus's image that describe the Savior, each one defining his character, but more importantly, illustrating the image we should strive to hold.

We've also been reminded of the image the world says we should portray. Unfortunately, Christ's image and the world's image couldn't be any more different.

But here's where the rubber meets the road: *How do we change our image to look like his?*

How do we put down our checkbook and pick up our cross? How do we keep from obsessing over pulling off the pounds but pulling off our sin? How do we quit worrying about degrees and start worrying about discipleship?

As we begin this fourth chapter that strives to answer these critical questions, I'll offer a few tips that have helped me.

1. *Humility*

We want to be the image of the invisible God, but we can't do it without humble hearts. One day, a preacher went to visit an expert farmer, who had just bought a farm that had been in ruins for years. The soil was covered with weeds, the barns were falling down, and the snake infested tanks were caramelized with cobwebs. When the preacher arrived, the farmer met him on the front porch. The preacher couldn't believe it. In just a matter of weeks, this farmer had planted crops in fresh turned soil, he had rebuilt the barns, and the tanks were full with purified, crystal clear water. The preacher told the farmer, "My goodness son, you and the Lord have done wonders with this place!" The farmer replied, "You should have seen it when the Lord had it by himself!"

Obviously, the farmer didn't get it. Sure, he worked hard day and night, and his expertise certainly improved the farm's appearance, but the farm was only transformed by God's power working through him!

Our personal transformation with God works the same way. We must be involved and dedicated to the challenge. However, at the end of the day, it's only because God allowed the transformation to occur.

2. *Perseverance*

You've probably experienced a diet program. You start out strong for the first few weeks, and you can feel yourself starting to trim, but after a while, your dedication begins to die. Food starts to taste the same. Exercise becomes boring. Saying no becomes more challenging and dissatisfying. Before you know it, not only have you given up the diet, but you've probably put back on the weight you lost, if not more.

Reflecting the image of the invisible doesn't just happen. It's a very difficult task, and as soon as our commitment begins to waiver, Christ's image begins to fade into the distance. Very soon, we find ourselves further and further from the image that defines who we are. To draw us back, it takes earnest, sincere perseverance.

3. *Patience*

"All good things take time." We don't rise to the top of our careers quickly. We don't enter retirement after two months of employment. We don't develop a strong reputation without years of proving ourselves. If we want it, we can get it but only if we're patient.

Becoming the image of the invisible can't be done overnight. King Solomon once wrote, "He has made everything beautiful in its time" (Ecclesiastes 3:11, NIV). Solomon wasn't joking. He wrote those words from experience, and he knew that without the passing of time, beauty won't come.

Take a deep breath and get ready for your life to be changed forever. But remember, if you truly want to reflect Christ, you must reflect him with *humility*, *perseverance*, and *patience*.

Even if you have humility, perseverance, and patience, you still need a vision. The changes you make *today* will reflect Christ's image *tomorrow*. Consider these passages.

Romans 12:1–2

Let's start with a very broad scope of reasoning. In his letter to the church at Rome, Paul gave some great advice on how to "start over."

Have you ever noticed that when we realize something must change, *making* the change is harder than realizing the change is needed?

You say you're going to save money, but what happens when you see that item you just have to have? You say you're going to learn to say no to your children, but what happens when you hear those young, innocent words, "Daddy, please?" Saying that something needed to change was as easy as pie, but when it came time to make the change, the pie wasn't as easily swallowed.

But Paul tells us how to conquer the challenge.

> Therefore, I urge you, brothers in view of God's mercy, to offer your bodies as living sacrifices, holy and pleasing to God—this is your spiritual act of worship. Do not conform any longer to the pattern of this world, but be transformed by the renewing of your mind. Then you will be able to test and approve what God's will is—his good, pleasing, and perfect will. (Romans 12: 1–2, NIV)

Paul makes some powerful points.

1. *"Offer your bodies as living sacrifices, holy and pleasing to God."*
   Did Jesus imitate these words? Absolutely! Jesus was a "living sacrifice" for thirty-three years. His entire life prepared him for death. Through every message, through every action, Jesus promoted sacrifice. Words like "it's not the healthy who

need the doctor, but the sick," described his devotion to the less fortunate and afflicted. Personal remarks of ambition such as "the Son of Man did not come to be served, but to serve" illustrated his desire for social justice. Sacrifice. That's who Jesus was and what he was about.

2. *"Do not conform any longer to the pattern of this world, but be transformed by the renewing of your mind"*

This statement is critical. If we want to illustrate Christ, we must let go of the world. When Jesus said, "Do not be surprised if the world hates you" (John 16, NIV), it wasn't a suggestion or a whimsical catch on words. The world is supposed to hate you, and you are supposed to hate the world, not the individuals who inhabit it, but the grotesque sin, heartbreaking hypocrisy, and unnecessary pain that come therein.

It's impossible to please the world and please Christ. Jesus constantly said, "I have come to do the will of the Father." Isn't it interesting that Jesus never said, "I've come to make this world happy, turn heads, and impress with my charm"? That's because he knew the former was impossible with the latter.

This doesn't mean we should cocoon or barricade ourselves from the world God created—but it does mean we should realize who we are, and whose we are, so we can fulfill our responsibility as God's people. Paul reminds us to be transformed by the renewing of our mind. The only way to renew our mind is to reject the world's grip. Jesus did, and so should we.

3. *"Then you will be able to test and approve what God's will is—his good, pleasing, and perfect will."*

    Have you ever been involved in a debate about God's will? People wonder, "What does God want for my life?" Or "Why am I here?" Or "Is it God's will for me to take this job?" "Is it God's will for me to marry her?" All of these questions are reasonable and confusing.

We may never measure every inch of God's omnipotent will, but Paul tells us how to understand what we need to understand. He says, "Then you will be able to test and approve what God's will is" (Romans 12:2).

When does the "then" come into effect? When we become "living sacrifices" and refuse to "conform to the world"?

Give it some thought. Do you understand God's purpose for your life? Do you desire clarity about today and tomorrow?

Learn to sacrifice. Then you will be able to test and approve as you watch the world and its desires disappear through the rearview mirror.

Romans 6:1

Paul's instruction in Romans 12 concerning transformation is very broad. Transformation isn't a one time occurrence; transformation is a lifestyle. In Romans 6, Paul gives this specific plea for everyday life. He writes, "What shall we say, then? Shall we go on sinning so that grace may increase? By no means! We died to sin; how can we live in it any longer?" (Romans 6:1, NIV).

In the first century, Christianity was new and exciting. The idea of mercy and grace was cutting edge. People were captivated by the idea that their sin *could* and *would* be atoned for by one man's death from Nazareth.

The Jews were accustomed to rituals that required them to find an animal to make amends with God. But now, Jesus had taken care of it. He was the lamb that was slaughtered.

Sin? No big deal. God's grace was there.

What was Paul's reaction? "By no means!" Older translations even say, "God forbid!"

That's not the purpose of God's grace. God didn't give his one and only Son so we could have a good time. God gave Jesus because we can't survive without him.

With a gift of that caliber, something is required of us.

Unfortunately, we still miss the mark today. Even though thousands of years separate the cultures, we're the same people. We're selfish, unthankful, and extremely worldly. We seek any and every appetizing opportunity to give into the rampant desires of the flesh. We do what we want because we believe God's grace will cover it all, and in doing so, we cheapen the most valuable gift ever given to man.

I like to remember the value of grace through an acronym.

G od's
R iches
A t
C hrist's
E xpense

Does that make you think twice about the choices you make?

Does that make you carefully consider the magnitude of your sin?

Does that help you appreciate the meaning of Calvary?

Christ gave his life, so we could be found righteous before God. Don't make *Christ's* death a tragedy because *you* can't give everything to God. Christ gave his life for you. You can give your life for him!

1 John 2:6

It doesn't always require lengthy presentations and eloquent presenters. In fact, sometimes it's the simple geniuses that cut right to the chase, lay it out on the table, and pour truths into the mold. Simplicity is what cuts so deep.

When I think about a simple explanation for the image of the invisible God, I can't help but remember the few words from the apostle John in 1 John 2:6, "Whoever claims to live in him must walk as Jesus did" (NIV).

That's it. No dogmatic discussions about doctrine. No deep, unsolved, theological theories of scholars. Simple words with profound application—i*f you want to live in Jesus, you must walk like him!*

These words slice us all the way to the core because we probably realize vocal dedication is superficial compared to the steps we actually take.

How did *Jesus* walk?

We can't trace every step through the streets of Jerusalem, the quiet tranquility of Bethany, and the home town comfort of Nazareth, but we can summarize all his steps in this way—his steps were *by* the will of God, *for* the benefit of mankind. He was guided by God so he could serve others.

How do *you* walk?

Are your steps directed by the will of God so you can serve others? With each step, do you think him and them, or me and we?

When was the last time you went out of your way to do something kind for someone else? When was the last time you saw a friend hurting and hurt with them? When was the last time you wanted to be the solution rather than the problem?

Simply put, when was the last time you were the hands and feet of Jesus? If you claim to be in Christ, you will play that role.

You see, when Jesus said, "Come, follow me," he knew exactly what he was doing. Through his steps, smiles, and tears, he paved the paths that lead to eternal life.

If we're in him, we will *listen* when he says, "I am the way, the truth, and the life." (John 14:6, NIV). If we're in him, we will *believe* when he says, "No one comes to the Father except through me" (John 14:6, NIV). If we're in him, we will *follow* when he offers the invitation. If we don't, his visibility will be invisible in our lives.

Philippians 2:5–11

Roses are red. Violets are blue. Daddy sang bass. Momma sang tenor. Spare the rod. Spoil the child. The early bird gets the worm. No pain, no gain. Practice makes perfect.

These common phrases have survived the test of time.

Roses are red.

Violets are blue.

Words that have inspired every husband running late for Valentine's Day.

Daddy sang bass.

Momma sang tenor.

Words that can't help but make even the grumpiest of grumps sing.

Spare the rod.

Spoil the child.

Words that have caused the hottest debates and arguments among parents.

The early bird gets the worm.

Words that every procrastinator hates.

No pain, no gain.

Words that make exercise doable.

Practice makes perfect.

Words that leave us with hope but also without excuse.

It doesn't matter who we are or where we've been, at least one of those slogans hits home.

Why? Is it because they're so undeniably profound? Is it because they're unmistakingly correct?

No. It's because they're so easy to remember. And since they're easy to remember, they're easy to emulate.

In our struggle to change our image to Christ's image, the Bible offers catchy phraseology.

Even though the church at Philippi was a church that did many things well, they had their own challenges.

In the midst of their rejoicing, they tended to struggle with pride.

In fact, Paul mentions two women, Euodia and Syntche, who struggled to get along. Paul pleaded with them to "agree in the Lord" (Philippians 4:2, NIV).

Can you imagine sitting in that church at Philippi, listening to the letter being read by one of the members of the congregation, from the apostle Paul, and then hearing your named called out? "Oh ya, those two ladies Euodia and Syntche, can someone please tell them to stop their cat fights?" Wow, I think I would have crawled under the pew!

But as Paul addresses these issues of pride and arrogance, Paul says, "Do nothing out of selfish ambition or vain conceit, but in humility consider others *better* than yourselves" (Philippians 2:3, NIV).

Those words can be hard to hear.

"Consider others better than myself? But, Paul, don't you know them? Haven't you heard what they've done and what they're like? That they're rabble rousers? That they can't hold down a job? That they can't keep their promises? You want me to consider them *better* than myself? Paul, you can't be serious."

But Paul says, "Yes, I know them. And I am serious. In fact, this is how I want you to consider them better than yourself."

Image of the Invisible God

> Your attitude should be the same as that of
> Christ Jesus: Who, being in the very nature
> God, did not consider equality with God
> something to be grasped, but made himself
> nothing, taking the very nature of a servant,
> being made in human likeness. And being
> found in appearance as a man, he humbled
> himself and became obedient to death—even
> death on a cross.
>
> Philippians 2:5–11 (NIV)

It's called the Christ Hymn. In fact, it was sung as a song by churches in the first century during their worship, but it still changes and convicts us today.

Just look at the words.

"Your attitude should be the same as that of Christ Jesus."

Jesus loved the unlovable. He cared for the uncaring. He was hungry to help the hungry, and thirsty to help the thirsty. Is that your attitude?

"Did not consider equality with God something to be grasped." What? Why not? In our world, equality is a big deal. Regardless if it's our race, gender, or prestige, we all want to play on the same playing field. Not Jesus. Even though he was God, he said, "I'm okay being number 2. I'm okay dropping to the level of those I want to save."

"Taking the very nature of a servant."

If there ever was a *real* servant, it was Jesus. Washing feet? Absolutely not; not me. But for Jesus, washing feet wasn't just an act of love, it was a lifestyle. It was a dedication to a higher calling, a higher standard of living, and a higher purpose than even those whose feet were made clean.

"He humbled himself and became obedient to death, even death on a cross."

Jesus died on a cross we aren't even willing to carry. As painful as the nails and the crown of thorns were, Jesus experiences more pain when he sees us give up our calling of discipleship. If Jesus can become obedient to death, we can become obedient for life.

The Christ Hymn.

It's a real jingle if you ask me. But if we want our image to imitate the invisible, the Christ Hymn will be as common as roses are red, violets are blue.

Luke 23:24

The time had come. The knot was tangled in Jesus's stomach. Calvary was drawing nearer hour by hour, minute by minute, second by second.

All of Jesus's chosen ones had run away in fear. The Roman soldiers barged into the final meeting at Gethsemane, cuffed the Christ, and led him to his trial. When Jesus needed his followers the most, they were gone.

Surface statements like "we will go where you go" were quickly fading into the fog of rejection. Even Jesus's biggest supporter, Peter, had run away to his own, personal hideout. Well, he didn't run too far. He was still close enough to watch the events and hear the boisterous yells from the angry crowd. But as Peter warmed his hands over a fire making himself comfortable, he drew anything but comfort.

Just like Jesus had promised, even Peter denied Jesus three times, crying tears of bitterness after the deeds were done.

But after Jesus was found guilty for his innocence, Jesus put one foot in front of the other, every step with excruciating pain, and he walked that lonely road to his death.

And once again, he walked alone.

In the blink of an eye, Jesus was nailed to beams that would hold him for six agonizing hours. The crown of thorns that had already split his scalp cut even deeper, and the blood continued to pour down his face. With every inkling of his failing strength, Jesus gasped for air polluted by sin, as the nails continued to rip his flesh.

If you had been hanging on that cross for a group of people who not only rejected you, but *despised* you, what would you have said? "Get me down from here"? "This is wrong"? "Why are you doing this to me"?

But what did Jesus say? "Father, forgive them, for they do not know what they are doing."

Forgive them? They don't know what they're doing? Are you kidding?

Crucifixion was an art. Soldiers didn't just nail someone to a cross. It required strict training and practice. And not only did they have to learn how to nail a body to a cross, but they studied the precise location to nail, the exact angle to hang, the indefinite timing in which it needed to be done to cause the most pain.

Didn't know what they were doing? Jesus, they knew *exactly* what they were doing! They were crucifying you because in their eyes, you didn't deserve to live.

But Jesus looked beyond the hammers, blocked out the peer-pressured, cowardly orders from Pilate, and Jesus said, "Father, forgive them."

Can you imitate an image like that? Can you forgive those who are persecuting you? And not only persecuting you, but persecuting you *on purpose*?

I hope by the grace of God that I would, but I admit that I'm not sure I could. And once again, to be completely honest, I don't think I would have *wanted* to.

But there is one point that needs to be made about Jesus's forgiveness. God may not have expected *Jesus* to forgive in that moment, and he doesn't always expect *us* to forgive in the heat of calamity.

Jesus prayed, "*Father*, forgive them, for they do not know what they are doing." Jesus didn't say, "I forgive you," but Jesus prayed that *God* would grant the forgiveness. Jesus asked God to carry out Jesus's desire.

Many times in our lives, we may not have the strength to forgive. People have hurt us too much. They have pushed the buttons they knew not to push. They broke the promises they knew to keep. And we can't even imagine saying, "I forgive you."

Jesus showed us how. When we can't, God can. When we won't, God will.

But it's still up to us to pray that same prayer, "Father, forgive them."

You see, there are many ways we can change our image to look like his. From humility to transformation, from obedience to forgiveness, imitating Jesus requires spiritual dedication, but it's possible.

I never claimed it's easy. In fact, Jesus promised us it *wouldn't* be. Jesus said that in this world we will have many problems.

But just because we have problems, Jesus doesn't let us off the hook.

Will *your* image be *his* image? He still waits for you to change. So, my friend, do yourself a favor, and make the changes.

Discussion Questions:

1) Which passage in this chapter tugs on your heart strings the most? Why?

_____

_____

_____

2) In what ways have you failed to embody its message?

_____

_____

_____

3) Which passage do you find most relevant in your life, today?

_____

_____

_____

4) How will you embody its message tomorrow?

_____

_____

_____

Chapter Five

Portraying the Image

O ur journey through the image of God is beginning to make its final lap. Well, the journey itself isn't coming to a close, just the pages of this book.

This journey is a lifelong journey that continues through eternity. We're only touching the surface of one of scripture's most profound thoughts—*The Image of the Invisible God.*

Back in chapter 3, we discussed many of the images society tells us to portray.

Regardless if it's pulling off the pounds, building up the bank account, or getting that degree, the message is to become someone you aren't. Change who you are now because that change, how maximum or minimum it might be, will provide a bigger and better you.

Really? Are you sure?

That change is what's needed to fix your problems?

Will a thinner waistline save your struggling marriage?

Will a larger bank account improve your parenting?

Will that extra degree change someone's life and help them see the cross through the thick fog of materialism that hovers over our society?

Worldly images lack substance. They are simply Satan's lies, unfortunately often expressed by many who sincerely want to follow Christ.

They listen to the *world* rather than listening to the *Word*, and consequently, the images they strive to portray lack any religious substance or security.

Society says, "Buy the *biggest* home on the block. Drive the *fanciest* car. Wear the *flashiest* clothes."

Why? What's the purpose? What's the benefit? Is there any answer other than, "I'm concerned with what other people think about me"?

There's nothing wrong with being concerned about what other people think. In fact, that's a very biblical concept.

Peter told Christian women in his first epistle,

> Wives, in the same way be submissive to your husbands so that, if any of them do not believe the word, they may be won over without words by the behavior of their wives, when they see the purity and reverence of your lives. (1 Peter 3:2, NIV)

Peter wanted these wives to be very concerned about what their husbands thought about them. If these

Christian women lived Christ-like lives, Peter believed that through their godliness, they could encourage their unbelieving husbands to become believing, godly men.

So being concerned about what other people think is important, as long as we're concerned for the right reasons. Not so people will see how great *I* am, but so they will know how great my *God* is!

God, our Father, sends a different message about the image we should portray. It doesn't focus on what we can do, but what *he* can do through us. It's his image, not ours. But through our existence and presence in his world, we portray his image so the "invisible" will be visible.

As you strive to portray God's Image, the image by which *you* were created, remember these vital, scriptural recipes for success.

Matthew 5

I would have loved to have witnessed the Sermon on the Mount.

As a fellow preacher, I can only imagine the adrenaline that must have been pumping through Jesus's chest as he delivered a powerful sermon to the masses, sitting on the gorgeous green hills rolling to the shores of the Sea of Galilee.

There was no powerpoint. No cameras. No buzzing microphone with irritating feedback. No time limit.

There was only the Messiah, the true spokesman of God, bringing a powerful lesson to hungry hearers.

Today, we define the Sermon on the Mount as chapters 5–7 in the Gospel of Matthew. During this sermon, Jesus touched on some pretty heavy issues.

He gave nine Beatitudes that informed people how they would live if they achieved their purposes. Jesus said, "You will be blessed" if you do these things. Not necessarily happy but *blessed*—better tomorrow; stronger today.

Jesus spoke out against murder, adultery, divorce, hatred, and many other worldly sins of the flesh.

Jesus told us to care for those who are less fortunate. Jesus showed us how to pray. Jesus told us how to fast. Jesus told us where our treasure should be, which looks nothing like Wall Street. Jesus told us "not to worry," for if we "ask, seek, and knock," we will find what we're looking for.

But unlike other preachers who are "booed" out of the auditorium when they say "one last point," and then proceed to make seven more, Jesus captivated his audience. It didn't matter if it was thirty minutes or thirty hours, the crowd was there to stay.

But during this life-changing speech, Jesus also touched on the purpose of this chapter, how to "portray our image."

Jesus said,

> You are the light of the world. A city on a hill cannot be hidden. Neither do people light a lamp and put it under a bowl. Instead they put it on its stand, and it gives light to everyone in the house.

> (Matthew 5:13–14, NIV)

Two metaphors: "light of the world" and "city on a hill." I'm not sure if Jesus intended to create two metaphors for portraying an image, but for our purposes, let's look at them separately.

For hundreds and hundreds of years, the church has served as a city on a hill. Granted, the church has made many mistakes that have caused it to be viewed as a prison or dungeon or club, rather than the welcoming, warm, hospital that it really is.

However, no one can argue that the church has grabbed people's attention.

People know that the church exists. It's a city on a hill that's impossible to miss. Why? There is power in numbers and influence.

But it's the *second* metaphor which Jesus mentions *first* that's so difficult to portray—light of the world. Light is one of the strange mysteries of life. It has progressed from the friction of wood, to the strike of a match, to the flip of a switch. Today, we know that light travels at one hundred eighty-six thousand miles per second. Jesus really used a timeless illustration.

But Jesus didn't just speak of light. Jesus said, "You are the Light of the World."

Not just in your corner. Not just in your cubicle. Not just in your church. Everywhere you go, you are light to the world around you. To people you know, and people you may never meet.

How is that reasonable? How is that logical? Who cares? It's possible.

I think I truly appreciated Jesus's emphasis on light for the first time when I lived in Llano, Texas. It was my first preaching job. My wife and I had been married for two weeks, and we had just graduated from college two months before when we loaded up the moving truck and headed for the thriving metropolis of Llano, the Deer Capital of Texas.

There were many reasons why Llano was proud of its nickname. The deer brought many hunters to the area every year. The deer were fun to watch. The deer reminded us we weren't alone.

But the real reason I think Llano was so interested in their legacy? There were more deer than people.

Llano was a very small town in the beautiful Texas Hill Country. From my office, which was thirty steps from our home because we were living in the church parsonage, I could mail a letter, eat lunch, go to the courthouse, hardware store, and fire department, in less than a quarter of a mile. That's right, my wife and I moved to Mayberry!

But our time in Llano helped shape our marriage and helped shape my ministry. The lessons I learned there are irreplaceable.

Since Llano was so small, we would have to drive forty miles each way to a bigger town for Walmart. In fact, Walmart runs turned into date night for the first year of our marriage. We couldn't wait to go and see what other people were doing in that "other civilization" forty miles away.

We would often make these trips at night after I had finished my work day. Driving back through the pitch-black night in the hills of the desolate Texas Hill Country can be a fairly hairy thing to do at times.

You constantly have to be on the watch for deer running across the road, and visibility is terrible. The only thing you can see are the gorgeous stars in the dark Texas sky.

One night, we were headed back to Llano, and we ran into a terrible thunderstorm. The wind was howling, the temperature was dropping, and the rain was coming down in sheets.

Even though it was only a forty-mile trek, I feared our safety and anxiously waited till we could be back in our home, safe, sound, and dry.

I'll never forget the dim lights of Llano shining through the rain. The light wasn't strong or overpowering. It was a simple reminder that safety was close by.

That night, I felt closer to Jesus's sermon than I ever had before. It was exactly what Jesus had in mind. He wants us to be that light that represents safety, regardless how dim our light might be.

And you know, Jesus never told us, "You are the halogen of the world." Jesus never said, "Your light will overpower all other lights."

Jesus said, "You are the light of the world—so let your light shine."

There have been many times in my life where *my* light has flickered. It hasn't shined as strong as I would have liked or probably as strong as God would have liked, but nevertheless, it kept shining. The world still saw something—my God!

It doesn't matter if your light flickers or fosters, as long as it doesn't fail!

And Jesus tells us why it's so important in the next verse, "Let your light shine before men, that they may see your good deeds and praise your Father in heaven" (Matthew 5:16, NIV).

Our light doesn't shine for our glory, but for God's. To some, he might be invisible at first glance. But if our light continues to shine, that image will be as visible as the world around them.

"This little light of mine, I'm going to let it shine." I hope you'll join me.

1 Peter 2: 11-12

It's amazing that Peter, a man who was confident, yet also crooked at different times of his life, gives us amazing advice on how to portray the image of God.

As he was writing to young, persecuted, Christ followers, Peter said this:

> Dear friends, I urge you, as aliens and strangers in the world, to abstain from sinful desires, which war against your soul. Live such good lives among the pagans that, though they accuse you of doing wrong, they may see your good deeds and glorify God on the day he visits us. (1 Peter 2:11–12, NIV)

Aliens? Really? Aliens? Peter wants us to appear as green, slimy figments of imagination with heads nine times the size of our bodies?

Cool it with the spaceship and UFOs. Peter isn't wanting us to be solar, just strange—different than the world around us.

You see, the people who inhabit this world are created in the image of God, but sadly, the world itself looks nothing like its Creator.

We are consumed and absorbed with sin. Holiness is a very distant concept—something only *aliens* would achieve.

Peter says that we need to "abstain from sinful desires." Well, that doesn't sound like the world we know. That doesn't look like the things we see or the air we breathe. We've lost touch with God and his desires for us.

Paul told the church at Ephesus that "among you there must not be even a hint of sexual immorality, or any kind of impurity" (Ephesians 5:3, NIV). Listen, we don't just have hints of sexual immorality; we have the whole puzzle, and we think we've solved it.

Celebrities and athletes become more famous if they're more immoral. Infidelity is a metaphor for big money and primetime.

Somewhere along the way, we missed it. No, we didn't just miss it—we ignored it.

That little voice (that most call the conscience) said, "You're going the wrong way, turn around," but society laced up its sneakers and continued the journey.

And where has it got us? The world that you and I know—full of immorality, full of idolatry, full of insecurity and infidelity, but lacking the "image" we need to portray.

It's time to turn around. It's time to listen to Peter. Maybe we should board our spaceship. Whatever it takes, it's time to once again be aliens—be different than the world around us.

Now, don't get me wrong, if we do board that spaceship, that doesn't mean we can fly away to a more secure, classified area. As aliens, we must still live among earthly creatures and be influenced by earthly ways. But as we live on this earth that is not our own, we must live "good lives among the pagans" (1 Peter 1:12, NIV).

These good lives aren't for *us*; these good lives are for *God*. You see, Jesus and Peter had the same idea.

Jesus said, "Let your light shine (portray your image) so that people may see your good deeds and glorify God in Heaven" (Matthew 5:16, NIV).

Peter said, "Live such good lives among the pagans (portray your image) that, though they accuse you of doing wrong, they may see your good deeds and glorify God on the day he visits us" (1 Peter 1:12, NIV).

The image we portray, we portray for God. After all, it is *his* image, and as people created in that image, we are the venues to make the invisible, visible.

Be light. Be aliens. Live good lives. To God be the glory.

Jacob Hawk

Discussion Questions:

1) Has your light ever "flickered"? Has it ever burned out? Why?

_____

_____

_____

2) How will you not only make your light shine brighter, but forever?

_____

_____

_____

3) Does this world feel like your home? Why, or why not?

_____

_____

_____

4) In what ways will you become more like an "alien"?

_____

_____

_____

Chapter Six

Keeping the Image

I hope you've enjoyed our journey. These pages have attempted to wrap our minds around the divine, eternal concept of the image of the invisible God.

We've defined Jesus's image. We've described the world's image. We've considered ways to change our image to be like his and how we portray that image once we've changed accordingly.

But now, the task is in your hands—how do you *keep* that image? As our journey concludes together, remember these key tips to make it possible.

Exercise

This is no stranger to American culture. Any given night of the week gyms are packed with adults trying to burn off those calories so they can look better and be more efficient in the workplace.

Companies like Nike and Reebok have made a fortune from fitness-minded people. It's ironic that even though America is one of the most obese countries in the world, it also has the most exercisers. Go figure.

People exercise in different ways. They might join a gym, hire a trainer, or develop their own programs on their own time, but regardless of the method they choose, they have the same goal—get moving.

Get off the chair and get on the treadmill. Switch your spot on the couch for a spotter lifting weights. Run the court, not the kitchen.

Keeping the image of God works the same way—it's dependent on spiritual exercise.

James, the brother of Jesus, hit the nail on the head when he wrote in James 2:14, "What good is it my brothers, if a man claims to have faith but has no deeds? Can such a faith save him?" (NIV).

The answer is obviously no. If you want to keep reflecting the image of God, it takes action.

In my life, I've known many people who have fallen victim to lethargic spirituality. They were the people who said, "Yes, I have faith," but they lacked the godly proof to support their spiritual claims.

I once sat down with an older gentleman who was criticizing younger members in our congregation for letting go of key, core values, that help design and build the church of the New Testament. He was a great brother in Christ with wonderful intentions, but unfortunately, he was missing the entire picture.

I asked him why he was concerned about these younger members, and after an hour of consulting and consoling, I realized it came back to the same premise— he believed they weren't working hard enough for our church.

According to him, they were the younger, more energetic ones. They should be carrying a heavier load. They should be leading programs and ministries with the backbone and passion that only comes from youth.

I listened to his thoughts with openness and genuine interest. After hearing the concerns of his heart, I then asked him some questions. Each time he criticized the younger generations, I responded with, "Yes, but what are you doing for the kingdom?"

It caught him off guard.

He continued to mention failed opportunities and laxadaziacal mind-sets of the younger members. I listened but asked him again, "Yes, but what are you doing for the kingdom?"

Once more, he dove into the problems and mishaps of those younger than him, who sat across the pew and neglected their responsibility. And then I asked again, "Yes, but what are you doing for the kingdom?"

After an hour of personal evaluation, he finally responded with the right answer, "Not as much as I can."

"Not as much as I can." It's the equivalent of not as much as I should, or better said, not as much as God has commanded.

We reflect God's image, and God is a God of action. As his image bearers, we must follow in his steps, constantly exercising that which we believe, say, and do.

Workout with Others

It's very difficult to be enthusiastic about exercise when you work out by yourself. It doesn't matter what's on the television, how nice the equipment might be, or how tasty the work out shakes are, working out by yourself is a drag. It makes all the difference when others are suffering alongside you.

My wife and I have been married for several years, but when we were students at Harding University, she would work out every day at the same time with her girlfriends.

Was it to stay in shape? Of course not. They were in great shape.

It was a social event called "meet boys." Luckily, she didn't meet any workout gurus that captured her heart.

I did workout every day my freshman year with my roommate. Sophomore year, he moved to a different dorm, and my workout routine suffered, and I don't mean a little bit—I mean drastically. I don't think I went once the entire year. Without him, working out wasn't the same.

Keeping God's image walks hand in hand with this undeniable truth.

You can't do it on your own. Sure, you might start out with a forty-yard dash. But over time, it turns into a run, into a jog, into a brisk walk, into strolling, until you finally quit. You need others to keep you motivated.

The best way for you to "workout with others" is to become involved in a local church.

The Hebrew writer was very clear about the importance of church life. He wrote in Hebrews 10:24–25 (NIV):

> And let us consider how we may spur one another on toward love and good deeds. Let us not give up meeting together, as some are in the habit of doing, but let us encourage one another, and all the more as you see the Day approaching.

Look carefully at those words: "let us," "spur," "encourage," and "all the more." That's what working out with others is all about.

God knew what he was doing when he designed the church. He knew we would need that encouragement and motivation, and we need to take advantage of such a wonderful blessing.

Many people are hesitant to become part of a church because they have been burned by organized religion. As a minister and church leader, if you fall into this category, I want to apologize for any experiences that you might have endured.

The Lord's church is supposed to be a hospital for those who are hurting, a school for those who want to learn, a safe haven for those who are living in fear, and a parade for those who need that push to do God's will on earth.

Granted, the church is made of people, and whenever people are involved, problems will occur. However, if you have left the church because of hurt feelings, disappointments, and the pain caused by hypocrites, I beg you to reconsider.

You truly are missing one of God's greatest gifts. You need the church, and the church needs you.

Finding that right church can be a very difficult task. It seems like there are as many churches as fast-food restaurants and coffee shops. All of them have a different mission, appearance, and vision.

As someone who has been active in church his entire life, and involved in church leadership for several years, I offer two recommendations for choosing a church that will never lead you wrong:

1. *Find a church that imitates the church described in the New Testament.*

    You will visit churches that operate very differently than the church written about in the New Testament. Study your Bible. Read the letters of the apostle Paul to various churches. Find one that passionately obeys God's word. How can a church go wrong doing what the Bible says? If you find a biblical church, you will find a *faithful* church.

2. *Find a church that expects you to be involved.*

    I chose these words carefully. I didn't say a church *where* you can be involved, but that *expects* you to be involved. Many churches have programs and ministries to offer. Few churches expect members to participate.

    This is what's called organic church, and the church of the New Testament was organic. Acts 2 describes the church of Jerusalem in this way,

    They devoted themselves to the apostles' teaching and to the fellowship, to the breaking of bread and to prayer. Everyone was filled with awe, and many wonders and miraculous signs were done by the apostles. All the believers were together and had everything in common. Selling their possessions and goods, they gave to anyone as he had need. Every day they continued to meet together in the temple courts. They broke bread in their homes and ate together with glad and sincere hearts, praising God and enjoying the favor of all the people. And the Lord added to their number daily those who were being saved. (Acts 2:42–47, NIV)

Find a church like that.

Granted, times are different. We don't sell all our possessions and meet daily, even though it would be great if we could, but that church in Jerusalem was involved in each other's lives, and they thrived. Scripture says, "The Lord added to their number daily."

Why? These new Christians "worked out with others" and when they did, keeping God's image was not only possible, but *popular*.

We probably have never met. I hope that by reading this book, you feel like you know me in one way or another.

As a man striving to keep the image of God, and as a minister of the gospel of Jesus Christ, I offer you an open invitation to visit the church I serve any Sunday.

When you come, introduce yourself, tell me you've read this book, and lunch will be on me.

I want you to be involved. I want to get to know you. I want to help you keep God's image, and I want you to help me do the same.

Eat Right

Every good exercise program is accompanied by an even better diet plan. That's because it's impossible to stay fit if we don't eat the right things.

No fried foods. No sweets. Nothing processed. Nothing enjoyable.

Lots of green vegetables. Lots of protein. Lots of flatulence.

Very little bread. Very little grain. Very little starch. Very little happiness.

Where Do I Sign Up?

Yes, that's the joys of eating right, and it's necessary if that slim waistline is our pot of gold at the end of the rainbow.

We can run miles, pump out hundreds of push-ups, endure the pain of thousands of sit-ups, but if we don't make a habit of putting the right fuels in our body, we can never be healthy.

And for most people, eating right is the worse of two evils!

It's fairly common to get into a groove at the gym and even learn to appreciate that extra sense of confidence and strength that comes from physical exercise—but learning to turn down the tasty, fatty foods? That's a different story.

No one in their right mind would choose cool, crunchy broccoli over a baked potato swimming in buttery, creamy goodness. But if one is really serious about staying lean and mean, eat the tree and run from the fun.

Keeping God's image works the same way. We have to eat right if we want to be spiritually healthy, and the food we put into our body is more influential than we realize.

As soon as Jesus was baptized, he went into the wilderness for forty days where he was tempted by Satan. During those five and a half weeks, Jesus didn't eat a thing. Talk about an enjoyable vacation.

Satan, with his usual creative coy, attacked Jesus where he was weak. He told Jesus, "If you are the Son of God, tell these stones to become bread" (Matthew 4:3, NIV).

Surely Jesus would. He was hungry! And being God in the flesh, Jesus had more power than any other human being on the planet—he could fix the problem, silence the growl of his hunger and cure the pain of his flesh with just a few divine words.

It was a pathetic attempt to flatter Jesus's power. Tell the stones to become bread and ooula—sourdough, pumpernickel, rye, or wheat, it's there for the taking!

But Jesus avoided Satan's desperate plea for the fall from perfection. Jesus looked at Satan and said, "It is written: 'Man does not live on bread alone, but on every word that comes from the mouth of God.'" (Matthew 4:4, NIV)

Come again? Man does not live on bread alone? The Son of Man, the Bread of Life, the House of Bread says that bread doesn't cut it? Correct.

Physical bread won't keep the soul travelling down the straight and narrow road that leads to heaven's doors but only the "spiritual" bread found in the pages of the Bible.

We can pray, sing, serve, listen, obey, and give all we want, but if we don't eat right with a true balanced diet, we cannot keep God's image. And that balanced diet is the word of God.

You can fashion the diet to your life in different ways. Design a convenient schedule for your daily demands. Listen to the Bible on your iPad or iPhone as you exercise. Listen to the Bible in your car as you drive to and from work. Whatever method you choose, make sure it's a *daily* affair.

Paul complimented the church at Berea in Acts 17 because they "examined the scriptures daily" (Acts

17:11, NIV). The Bereans got it right. They chose the right *food*. They disciplined themselves to the right *diet*. They became the right *people*.

Remember the words of Jesus. Imitate the discipline of the Bereans. Avoid the fatty food of lies. Avoid the processed food of the media. Avoid the downright junk of this world, and Satan, its master. Be nourished by the word daily.

Get Some Rest

As Americans, we don't understand the concept of rest. A key foundation to the American dream is that time is money.

Unfortunately, we believe we should spend as much time as we can making money and climbing the ladder of success. Consequently, before we know it, decades have passed, along with our physical health and stamina. And all the things we worked to enjoy, we're no longer able to enjoy. It's an unfortunate, vicious, all too common cycle.

In the Old Testament, the Israelites were commanded to rest one day a week. That day was known as the Sabbath.

In fact, observing the Sabbath was one of the Ten Commandments given to Moses on Mt. Sinai. In Exodus 20, God commanded Israel,

Remember the Sabbath day by keeping it holy. Six days you shall labor and do your work, but the seventh day is a Sabbath to the Lord your God. On it you shall not do any work, neither you, nor your son or daughter, nor your manservant or maidservant, nor your animals, nor the foreigner within your gates. For in six days the Lord made the heavens and the earth, the sea, and all that is in them, but he rested on the seventh day. Therefore the Lord blessed the Sabbath day and made it holy.

(NIV)

God was very serious about the Sabbath day.

Jews were not to do any work or physical exertion, and there was a specific reason. It wasn't so they could be lazy. It was so God's people would take time to remember God. God even went so far to say, "I took a day of rest when I created the earth—you should do the same."

As I mentioned before, we rarely take this time of rest. We work and work and work, and in doing so, we forget the one who gives us the ability.

If we do take a day of rest, it doesn't serve a purpose. It's because we have passed the city limits of exhaustion, and our bodies can't physically function. This is not what God had in mind.

You see, God didn't say, "Take a day of rest so you can sleep." God said, "Take a day of rest so you can think about me." If we don't, we will never be able to keep his image.

Find ways in your life that you can take a Sabbath, not for your own personal satisfaction, but so you can learn to focus on God. Look for those opportune times to sit and dwell on God's glorious creation. Seek out those blessed moments in prayer, when you can give him all of your attention and passion. As a family, come together without the distractions of the world and talk about spiritual things rather than worldly affairs.

It's vital to your spiritual health. It's mandatory to keep the image of God. And most of all, it's a God-given concept.

Define Goals and Determine Strategies

People don't fail because they lack the ability to succeed. People fail because they lack defined goals and the strategies necessary to accomplish them.

We see this all the time.

People begin diet programs with the fairy tale vision of knocking off all the pounds and fitting back into those stellar jeans from high school, but the passion to drop the inches and improve the cholesterol isn't all that it takes—it requires a strategic plan, detailing the steps to accomplish the endeavor.

Weekly weigh-ins. New recipes. Different exercises. Set boundaries. Without these goals, coupled with strategy, success isn't attainable.

New businesses pop up on every corner, all with the same passion of bringing in the famous American dollar. Some businesses do well and make a name for themselves. Some businesses shut their doors within a matter of months, as dust and cobwebs cover the dreams of what could have been. Why? Goals were never defined. Strategies were never developed.

No one sat down and said, "By this time, we will be grossing this amount of profit." Or "By this time, we will be tapping into this target audience." Or "By this time, we will be considering expansion in other areas of the city."

No, they began with desire but finished with heartache. If only they had defined their goals and developed their strategies things could have been different.

It's the same way with keeping the image of God. Yes, we were created in God's image, but we can't keep that image correctly if we don't define our goals and develop our strategies.

Maybe you have a goal of reading through the Bible to better understand God's will for your life. Great goal! What's the strategy? If you read three chapters a day and five chapters on Sunday, it can be done in a year. But if you say, "Well, I'll do it on my own time," it won't happen. Trust me. I've tried.

Maybe you want to convert one of your friends to Christ. Outstanding! What is your strategy? Possibly begin with a weekly Bible study about confession, repentance, and baptism for the forgiveness of sins. After these Bible studies, bring them with you to church every time you go. Get them involved in a ministry. Get them connected with a group of believers. The goal is powerful, and it carries out the Great Commission of the gospel to advance the kingdom's cause, but you need that strategy to make it a reality.

Maybe you want to improve your prayer life. Perfect. What's your strategy? Learn to completely open up to God and tell him everything that's on your mind. Make it a habit of praying in the morning, afternoon, and evening. Pray with your family, and seek accountablity for these sacred moments with God.

Maybe you want to improve your parenting or possibly even your marriage. Don't we all? You get the idea.

Talking about it won't get it done. Even dreaming about it won't produce the results. It takes strategy and pure dedication.

But after all, isn't the image of God worth it? If God created you in his image, certainly you can take his creation and make it the best it can possibly be.

Define goals. Determine strategies. Succeed. It's that simple.

Never Give Up

It's the last tidbit of advice I have to offer. You may not remember anything I've written in this entire book, but please remember this—*never give up on the image of God.*

You've already been created in God's image, and the image will never disappear, but it's up to you to be the real McCoy.

If somehow you've heard me say or imply throughout the book that the image of God is a simple affair, I sincerely apologize. Paul said that even Christ is the the image of the invisible God (Colossians 1:15, NIV). That's a key insight into the complexity of the matter.

Christ, the Son of God, the Messiah, the Anointed One was portraying God's image, but people didn't believe him.

The way, the truth, and the life stood in the midst of lost souls, but men like Pilate, who looked at truth directly in the face asked the question, "What is truth?" (John 18:38, NIV).

Pilate could have reached out and touched truth with his bare hands, but he missed it.

Jesus's own apostles couldn't get past the idea of a physical kingdom when Jesus talked about making everything new. They were waiting for Jesus to redeem Israel and serve as their King.

Jesus was their King. He would redeem Israel. But it wouldn't be done with a horse driven chariot and a crown of gold. It would be done by carrying a cross and wearing a crown of thorns.

Judas missed it.

The Pharisees missed it.

I've missed it.

That's right, as a minister of Jesus Christ, I admit that I haven't always been what God has asked of me, and I still struggle to be what God expects of me.

I'll own up to it. I've polluted the image of God, just like everybody else.

At times, I fail to truly humble myself to the omnipotent power of God.

I have failed to trust in Jesus.

I have failed to accept and appreciate the image of the invisible God.

And since I have failed to accept it, trust it, and see it, I have failed to *keep* it.

But I don't give up. I keep pressing on.

I remain in the reach of grace, and I remain in the Savior's love.

And I know that if I continue to fight the good fight, and finish the race, there lies in store for me the crown of righteousness.

And that crown isn't just for me. That crown is for *you*, if the image of the invisible God defines the purpose of your life.

Winston Churchill once said, "Never. Never. Never give up."

To his adage, I add the truth of the gospel. God doesn't give up on you. Don't give up on him.

For you, my friend, are the image of the invisible God.

Discussion Questions:

1) Which tip in this chapter will you use the most to "Keep the Image"?

   _____

   _____

   _____

2) With whom will you "workout"?

   _____

   _____

   _____

3) What new "fuels" will fill your body?

_____

_____

_____

4) What goals do you have, and what strategies will you use to accomplish them?

_____

_____

_____

5) Today, tomorrow, and forever, how will you be the "Image of the Invisible God"?

_____

_____

_____